Baker the Financial Bear: Putting Money into the Piggy-Bank

Written by
Ian McDaniels

Illustrated By
Prea Davis

To my parents, teachers, and illustrator for helping me along the way

There lived a Butterfly who flew in the sky. This Butterfly always had enough money to purchase her favorite food: banana cream pie.

One day, the hungry Butterfly went to the store to order more. The store owner sadly shook her head and said to the Butterfly, "I am sorry, you can not have another banana cream pie. You do not have any more money."

The Butterfly thought she was sleeping since she was never denied her favorite pie. But eventually, she realized she was no longer dreaming, but instead weeping.

Unable to eat more pie, the Butterfly looked for money in Singapore, Ecuador, and even El Salvador. Without luck, the Butterfly was going to stop until she spotted her best friend Duck playing with bamboo in Peru.

"Quack! Quack!" said the Duck. I do love this hearty snack. The Butterfly asked the Duck for money, but the Duck did not have anymore. The Duck told the Butterfly to search elsewhere, even the sea.

The Butterfly flew in the sky to search the sea. The Butterfly even searched the nearest palm tree. The Butterfly flew, flew, and flew until the Butterfly saw her friend Bee.

Like the Duck, the Bee did not have any leftover cash. The only thing the Bee had was a mustache.

The Bee did not have anything to give the Butterfly but to tell the friend "to search elsewhere." The Bee recommended that the Butterfly should search even the air.

The Butterfly flew in the air until she could see her friend Bear. The Bear was relaxing on a sunny beach while eating a peach.

The Bear loved eating food, even seafood. The Butterfly interrupted the Bear's lunch and asked, "can I have some money to buy my favorite banana cream pie?"

Confused, the Bear asked, "why do you need money from me, did you ever save money in your piggy bank?" The Butterfly responded with a "no."

The Bear pulled out his piggy bank and told the Butterfly, "I always save my money in this piggy bank." The Butterfly asked, "why?"

Then, the Bear broke into song:
Everyone uses a piggy bank too,
To buy brand-new shoes,
Even some cool new toys,
That always brings me joooooooy,
Everyone needs a thing,
To ensure that everyone lives just like kings,
Don't go away,
You'll need a piggy bank to have a great daaaaay!!!

Baker, the bear, told the Butterfly to turn upside down because what he was going to say to her will turn into a smile from a frown.

The Bear told the Butterfly, "If you want to find more money, then you have to work hard." The two of them found money in weird places, even outer space.

Baker, the bear, told the Butterfly that, "you can collect coins from all kinds of events. Where you can use the money to go camping and even to buy a tent."

The Bear even told the Butterfly to save money from her gifts in her piggy bank to buy all new dolls.

Saving money ensures you get what you want, like eating banana cream pie at a restaurant. Instead of having no money to buy nothing, the piggy bank ensures that you always have enough money to buy something.

And the two of them broke into song again and sang:
    Everyone uses a piggy bank too,
    To buy brand-new shoes,
    Even some cool new toys,
    That always brings me joooooooy,
    Everyone needs a thing,
    To ensure that everyone lives just like kings,
    Don't go away,
    You'll need a piggy bank to have a great daaaaay!!!

After their adventure together, the Bear helped the Butterfly save money in her piggy bank to buy her favorite food: banana cream pie. With the saved money in the piggy bank, the Butterfly thanked the Bear with honey and even bought Baker a brand-new coffee maker.

Made in the USA
Middletown, DE
16 October 2020